Poems From the Heart

Joel Williams

PUBLISHED BY

Vabella Publishing

PO Box 1052

Carrollton, Georgia 30112

COPYWRITE © 2023 by JOEL WILLIAMS

All rights reserved. No part of this publication may be produced, stored in a retrieval system, or transmitted in any form by any means such as: electronic, mechanical, photocopying, recording, or otherwise, without prior permission from the author.

ISBN: 978-1-957479-56-9

PRINTED IN THE UNITED STATES OF AMERICA

DEDICATION

This book is lovingly dedicated
to my daughters,
Lori and Macy.

ACKNOWLEDGEMENTS

Many people contributed to the publication of this book. I want to share their names and their contributions. I'll begin by thanking my wife, Jeannie, who made the mistake of saying my first poem was "very good." That immediately, in my mind at least, put me in the category with Frost, Longfellow, and Yeats. She kept saying "very good" so I kept writing. Her contribution was not complaining too much about missing peaceful sleep as I tend to write best late into the night . . . in bed.

I owe much of the inspiration for this work to family and friends, especially for the ever-present thoughts of my grandchildren, Ashley, Jake, and Baylor. The loss of their Moms was devastating and the way they all managed that loss was truly inspiring. A number of the poems reflect that loss and will, hopefully, help someone in the same situation.

Beverly Bruemmer, mentor and big stick wielder to many aspiring writers, deserves my undying gratitude for getting the ball rolling and keeping it rolling. Her reminders, prods, and encouragements appeared randomly on my emails.

Many thanks for that, Bev, and for introducing me to Amber Pickle, an editor who is so adept at finding all the mistakes in grammar, punctuation, and style that I make due to having forgotten all that stuff I was supposed to learn in high school and college. Amber has also made helpful suggestions on word choice and finding graphics to accompany each poem. Thanks again, Amber and Beverly.

And finally, thanks be to God, for I have tried to put on paper the words He put in my heart.

PASSING THROUGH

"Pardon me," said the old woman
as she shuffled through the train.
"I'm just passing through," she mumbled.
Other riders showed disdain.

She must have carried all she owned
in the bag she held onto.
I thought of the words she said,
"I'm just passing through."

She waited for the doors to part,
then stole into the night.
I felt compelled to follow her
and inquire of her plight.

But I did nothing;
turned my eyes back to the news.
Still, my mind was addled;
wondering how many passing throughs
I'd failed to realize
were there, not just by chance,
but there to entrust me
to ease their circumstance.

How often in the past
did I fail to heed
a subtle urge to help
a passer through in need?"

"I'm too busy," I would often say,
"Let them take care of their own.
I don't have time for this.
Why can't they leave me alone?"

But the old woman's face
hovered in my restless mind
and I couldn't shake the thought
that I had been so blind.

We aren't here to amass personal wealth
or force our will on others.
We're here as part of God's plan
to be sisters and brothers.

We'll one day stand in His court
and answer face to face
"Did you feed my sheep,
or did you fame and fortune chase?"

I'm thankful for the old woman,
though I'm sure she never knew
that she made me realize
that we're all just passing through.

LEAVE SOMETHING

Poets are dreamers, artists with words.
They write odes and sonnets galore,
but their sentences in iambic pentameter
the average reader deems a bore.
But the odes and sonnets are grand
for those who understand
and the poet leaves a thing of beauty
for that is the poet's duty.

Artists are dreamers, artists with colors;
though many wind up boozers.
But their canvases in splendid array
decry their critical accusers
and the artist leaves a thing of beauty
for that is the artist's duty.

Dancers are dreamers, artists in motion,
incessantly practicing pas de duex.
But this keeps them in skinny shape
to get in their tights and tutus.

But their movement on stage
is quite often the rage,
and the dancer leaves a thing of beauty
for that is the dancer's duty.

Musicians are dreamers, artists in tones,
whose combinations may confuse or astound.
But despite the listeners' moans and groans,
the musician is pleased with her sound.
So fie with the audience's hisses,
the musician just blows them kisses
And the musician leaves a thing of beauty,
for that is the musician's duty.

Now, you are a dreamer, artist of something,
for all are endowed with a gift.
But nourishing a gift first means sowing
for its beauty to please and uplift.
So, search for that gift in your heart,
nourish it into an art,
then find its better to give than receive;
leave something beautiful when you leave.

YE WHO ARE WEARY

I couldn't understand why you had to go away.
I gave you life but you gave me being.
You gave everyone around you being.

You worked tirelessly for home, school,
and community.
Your legacy lives long in the hearts of those
who knew you.

But you worked beyond the limits of what your
tired and battered heart could endure.
Now I understand.

Christ said, "Come unto me all ye who labor and
are heavy laden. I will give you rest."
Rest well, my sweet daughter.

LOVE

If I could write of love, as did Shakespeare or Paul,
and have the words on callous hearts fall,
I'd try to persuade with lofty sentence
that hearts deny not loves existence.

Many questions does love beget
of dalliances, heartache, and regret.
What is love that blinds the lovers' reason?
Does love last forever or only for a season?

Does love not have eyes to see,
or is its blindness a casualty
of those who waited far too long,
and feared that love for them was wrong?

Who could fathom loves facets
and fail to respond to its giddy assets?
Who could scale its depth or height
and still not bask in pure delight?

Only those, it's feared, whose hearts were lured
into love, falsely, and find their hearts now inured.
May those in search of the lover's grail
taste the intoxicating ale.
May their hearts with romance fill
and their lips it's nectar swill.

Let love's path lead to verdant dales
and up precipitous hillside trails
to treat the naysayer's loveless gloom
with the ecstasy of love in bloom.

Love needs no self-defense;
it argues its own suspense
by gently tugging at emotions,
or filling hearts with illustrious notions.
Love's noble feelings should be lustily courted,
and plebeian sentiments carefully exhorted.

Some would question, "Why beckon heartbreak?
Does love hurt just for love's sake?"
But love may conquer or love may fail.
If it's strong or if it's pale
is determined by love's desirer,
or sadly, by love's denier.

So let not fear of love be your boast.
Taste the wine of love and toast
the delicacies of romance
and chance the possibility
that your heart will dance.

Joel Williams

GRANDSON

Thank you for the hug, grandson.
My heart needed a hug.
My life is painted in autumn hue
but my blood lives in you.
My race is nearly run.

You have blessed my very soul
for you bear the likeness of your mom.
I saw her spirit reflected in you
and as I watched you grow, I knew
her love for you made her whole.

I have you to thank, grandson,
for being her brightest star
and giving her life immense joy.
You were always her precious boy
and that, my grandson, can never be undone.

BALLERINA

I used to be a ballerina... twirling, leaping, soaring.
To be loosened from earth... twirling, leaping, soaring.
Followed by spotlight, the audience roaring.

I used to be a ballerina... before... before... It!
Sometimes... it's hard to think about... it...;
the crash, the drunken driver, the moment I was hit.

They said I would never dance again,
never know that freedom again,
and they couldn't heal the mental pain.

The pain of dreams torn and shattered.
Dreams toiled for but torn and shattered,
bits and pieces on the floor spattered.

How can one tolerate mere existence?
Living without dreams is mere existence.
Fighting self-destruction becomes the resistance.

How can one dance confined to a chair?
a chair with wheels, never-the-less a chair.
Is there a loving God somewhere?

Gone is the magic of the stage.
Gone are the sounds and lights of the stage.
In their stead, memories locked in a cage.

New paths must now be explored.
New ways of dealing must be explored.
Faith in life must be restored.

The world goes by, oblivious to my plight.
Oh, it paused briefly, then turned from my plight.
New dancers vied for my spotlight.

The scrapbooked playbills I open to remind me,
and faded newspaper clippings are there to remind me
of the art that once defined me.

To trade dreams in the middle of a dream
is to deny the soul a fulfilling dream
and force on the dreamer an alternate theme.

A new life direction with reduced zeal,
remaining years searching for the same zeal
that inflamed the heart when life was real.

. . . I used to be a ballerina . . .

SHE SLEEPS ON THE WIND

She slides down rainbows and splashes the puddles.
Every stray kitten, she gathers and cuddles.
She runs through fields and skips through meadows;
basks in sunshine but casts no shadows.

She's everywhere and nowhere, always around,
but distant, silent, waiting to be found.
You might catch a glimpse in a firefly's beam.
Was that really her or only a dream?

She delights in the flowers where butterflies play,
but if her solitude is threatened, she fades away.
She dances on moonbeams at day's end,
and closing her eyes, she sleeps on the wind.

CHRISTMAS ROSE

As a rose among the thorns,
    Christ the Lord on earth was born.
As the rose does love the vine,
    Christ the Lord does love mankind.

As the rose springs from the earth,
    Christ the Lord bore lowly birth.
As the rose does seek the sky,
    Christ the Lord now reigns on high.

The Christmas Rose blooms tonight
    'midst Angel Song and Holy Light.
The Christmas Rose blooms today
    where cattle low and oxen lay.

How sweetly smells the morning air
    'round the rose that grows so rare.
How beautiful the love that grows
    in those who find the Christmas Rose.

As the rose comes from the bud,
   eternal life comes from the blood.
As a fount it freely flows
   from Jesus Christ, our Christmas Rose.

The Christmas rose blooms tonight
   'midst Angel Song and Holy Light.
The Christmas Rose blooms today
   where cattle low and oxen lay.

How sweetly smells the morning air
   'round the rose that grows so rare.
How beautiful the love that grows
   in those who find the Christmas Rose.

How beautiful the love that grows
   in those who find the Christmas Rose.

MACY'S SONG

You were the symphony I could never write,
though your melody was in my head;
twirling, whirling in fanciful flight.
The harmonies of your soul, instead,
never revealed their inner feelings
and grew ever dissonant within
a troubled soul, reeling against
some imaginary, nonexistent sin.

Your opus would have been the coronation
of instruments and voices;
a ninth like Ninths that on occasion
have transcended human sources.
I could not write the rondo,
the usual refrain
with its lusty tempo
that the audience acclaims.

My pen would not leave the adagio
that seemed to pace your soul
and I longed to write your song, although
your absence took its toll.

I should have listened to you more;
studied the harmonies you created.
But my style came long before ,
and sadly, seemed outdated.

But I mourn for you, sweetheart,
that the world will never cheer
the symphony; that art,
that now only you can hear.
And I mourn for the way you left.
The loss has frayed my soul
and I am bereft
of what used to make me whole.

And should I collect the clutter in my head;
sort out the "what ifs" and "whys,"
then I'll recall the things you said
that would help me realize
the depression, the melancholy, the mood
that drove you to a sudden death
and quelled the music you knew.

The solitude now takes my breath
and pings that empty hole.
And I long for that melody
that could warm my frigid soul.

I'll use that theme, my love,
and write your symphony.
The heavens above
will declare that destiny
was prophetic all along;
and the world will someday know Macy's song.

HIDING FROM GOD

I tried to hide in the valley, He found me there.
As I fled into the forest, He saw my despair.
I scaled the mountain to its peak
and heard His voice above me speak,
"I can find you where e'er," He said.

"I designed this world. I fed
the seas with river streams
and set the moon amidst its beams.
I designed that forest glade.

"I know every mountain that I made
and every valley in between,
every rut, and each ravine.
So, hide from me if you think you must
to fulfill your sense of wanderlust.

But in the course of your travels,
when troubles loom and life unravels,

cry unto me and I will surely provide
you comfort. I'll walk by your side."

So now I'm found in God's embrace;
a place that's safe and filled with grace.
There's no cause for me to hide
for where I walk, God walks beside.

ENCORE

Ah! Little bird, who heard your song?
Amidst the din and clamor,
who heard the turn of a subtle cadence
on which you've worked so long?

Did anyone ask for another refrain
or shout, "Bravo, encore?"
Did they ask for another tune
or were your melodies in vain?

No! Little bird, I happened along.
I stood and heard your singing.
You see, we both were made musicians
and God gave us our song.

ON THE LOSS OF A CHILD

Questions burn unsatiated in the head,
swirling like an eddy in a pool,
sucking fallen leaves to their doom,
their grave a watery bed.

Questions, however, rise repeatedly
from the eddies of the mind.
They slink back to the starting gate
to refresh their assault more heatedly.

But the mind of a grieving dad
besieged by a 'What could I have done?'
Gloom desperately seeks comforting answers
but none are to be had.

And the distraught mom, hounded by constant, 'Whys?'
cannot find a restful moment
from unwelcome melancholy,
or control the tears that well her eyes.

How can parents, after the loss of a child,
climb from the pit of despair
that swallowed them like a sinkhole,
tho' safe paths of passage beguiled.

And lives rent by traumatic upheaval
cannot help but ponder the question,
"Can this be a part of God's plan,
or only a facet of good versus evil?"

Attempts at solace from family and friends,
although well-meaning and appreciated,
often dissolve into platitudes
for fear of spoken words that offend.

For the suffering parent has an addled mind
that focuses on loss and grief.
And though the face may exhibit a smile,
the inner psyche is mentally blind.

The loss of a child by a self-inflicted wound
is likened to a stab to the parents' hearts;
an act that shocks the purposeful mind
and keeps its mental branches pruned.

"What demons besieged this child of mine?"
the grieving parents ask.
"How could I have been so blind
to miss a warning sign?"

What did I do or fail to do
that could have prevented this destruction?
And the guilt that floods the parents' minds
crushes the sanity and distorts the view.

Time, and God, and sustaining friends,
may narrow the bottomless hole
that permeates the grieving heart.
But the hole, though narrowed, never ends.

So may your family live the natural order of life
where children outlive their parents;
for the grief over the loss of a child
slices the heart with a jagged knife.

REACHING FOR A STAR

If you only touch the moon when reaching for a star,
and you think of giving up because the star
is way too far, then gather up some moon dust
and put it in a jar.

If the trek thus far has really tired you out,
and the quest for the star is now in doubt,
ask yourself again what the star was all about.

Let the moon dust remind you how far you've come
as you look back from the moon and tally the sum
of the few who have conquered the moon's sanctum.

For the moon has been touched only by a few
whose spirit reflects a relentless view
to provide ensuing travelers a point to rendezvous.

So, the ones who have reached the moon before
knew their journey was to open another door
as a portal that star seekers may explore.

And view your efforts to reach for a star
as an offering to lower the bar
for those who seek to travel far.

To touch the moon is a noble feat
and many who attempt it succumb to defeat,
and in mid-journey, stumble and retreat.

So, celebrate your journey thus far
and let that moon dust in your jar
remind you that you reached for a star.

FIELD OF STONE

Fields of stone, cut and hewn
by seedlings, alive and warm.
With grieving hearts, they plant the fields
and weep their tears and mourn.

Fields of stone, the earth is laid,
the perpetual harvest hastening,
reaped by famines, wars, disease,
young buds the harvest wasting.

While the tears of the living fall on the dead
It's to our world their thoughts are giving . . .
How great must the tears of the dead
be falling for the living.

TWO WORDS

Wish I could hear them one more time,
those two words that flood my mind.
Like ghosts they haunt me through the night
and bid sweet sleep take its flight.

Sweet were the days when on the phone,
I marveled at the woman grown.
I marveled at her existence that lasted way
beyond prognoses of her day
when as a child she laid naked in a bed
with life machines beeping overhead
and tubes and needles in her hands.

So young she couldn't understand
the fear, the pain that made her cry.
Her frightened eyes asking, "Why?"

But miracle on miracle, God revealed
a new plan when prayers appealed
for life to linger further for her
to become wife and mother
and teacher, loving and fair to
all those who sat under her care.

But her own heart, weak and used,
though needing surgery, she refused.
She listened to her soul
and knew when life had reached its toll.

I would give all I have or ever had
to hear again those two words, "Hey, Dad."

MYSTERIES

I cannot fathom the mysteries of life
I am perplexed, bewildered
I sometimes think even mad.
They are often near.
I feel them close by!
One moment more and I can grasp ...
No ... No ...
Almost.

MONUMENT

Perhaps he stood before the hearth
at the close of a well-turned day,
turning his hands before the fire
in a reflecting, thoughtful way.
Perhaps he thought of the children in bed,
or the wife who stood beside,
his dreams yet further than ten years before
when he dreamed them to a young bride.
A two room house, he cut the logs,
the chimney he built with his hands.
Stand tall, young man, wherever you are,
your monument still stands.

ABOUT THE AUTHOR

Dr. Joel Williams' passion has always been music. He received Auburn University's first Master of Music degree, then moved his family to Tallahassee, Florida where he received a fellowship to teach while continuing his studies. He received his doctorate in music in 1986.

Tragedy struck Dr. Williams' family with the loss of his two daughters, one to heart disease, the other by self-inflicted wounds.

Years later, he turned his grief over to his creative mind and his book, Poems From the Heart, was born. Dr. Williams has proven himself to be just as talented in expressing what's in his heart through poetry as he is with music.

Dr. Williams is now retired from teaching and currently serves as pianist at Tabernacle Baptist Church. He resides in Carrollton, Georgia with his beautiful wife, Jeannie Hudson Williams, and enjoys family life with his stepchildren, and grandchildren.

Photograph by: Jeannie Williams

www.ingramcontent.com/pod-product-compliance
Lightning Source LLC
Chambersburg PA
CBHW020249010526
44107CB00002B/170